MATES
Peter Kenna

CURRENCY PRESS
The performing arts publisher

CURRENCY PLAYS

First published in 1996
by Currency Press Pty Ltd,
PO Box 2287, Strawberry Hills, NSW, 2012, Australia
enquiries@currency.com.au
www.currency.com.au

This edition published 2021

Copyright © The Estate of Peter Kenna, 2021.

COPYING FOR EDUCATIONAL PURPOSES

The Australian *Copyright Act 1968* (Act) allows a maximum of one chapter or 10% of this book, whichever is the greater, to be copied by any educational institution for its educational purposes provided that that educational institution (or the body that administers it) has given a remuneration notice to Copyright Agency (CA) under the Act.

For details of the CA licence for educational institutions contact CA, 11/66 Goulburn Street, Sydney, NSW, 2000; tel: within Australia 1800 066 844 toll free; outside Australia 61 2 9394 7600; fax: 61 2 9394 7601; email: info@copyright.com.au

COPYING FOR OTHER PURPOSES

Except as permitted under the Act, for example a fair dealing for the purposes of study, research, criticism or review, no part of this book may be reproduced, stored in a retrieval system, or transmitted in any form or by any means without prior written permission. All enquiries should be made to the publisher at the address above.

Any performance or public reading of *Mates* is forbidden unless a licence has been received from the author or the author's agent. The purchase of this book in no way gives the purchaser the right to perform the play in public, whether by means of a staged production or a reading. All applications for public performance should be addressed to Curtis Brown PO Box 19, Paddington NSW 2021, Australia, e-mail reception@curtisbrown.com.au

Typeset by Dean Nottle for Currency Press.
Cover design by Lisa White.

Currency Press acknowledges the Traditional Owners of the Country on which we live and work. We pay our respects to all Aboriginal and Torres Strait Islander Elders, past and present.

 A catalogue record for this book is available from the National Library of Australia

PETER KENNA was born in Balmain, Sydney, in 1930, one of thirteen children of a carpenter. He was educated at the Christian Brothers School, Lewisham, to the age of fourteen, after which he worked in a variety of jobs. By the 1950s he had become an established radio actor. Kenna first gained national attention as a playwright in 1959 when his third play, *The Slaughter of St Teresa's Day*, won the General Motors-Holden national playwrights competition, and was presented at the Elizabethan Theatre, Sydney. The play has since been widely performed on stage, radio and television in Australia and the United Kingdom.

Peter Kenna worked in London from 1960 to 1964 and *Talk to the Moon* was first presented at the Hampstead Theatre Club in 1963. After directing *Muriel's Virtues* in Sydney in 1966 he returned to London for extended treatment of a chronic illness. After settling again in Sydney in 1971 he had many stage productions: *Talk to the Moon* had its Australian premiere in Melbourne and *Listen Closely* in Sydney in 1972. His major play, *A Hard God*, had its premiere at the Nimrod Street Theatre, Sydney, in 1973, followed by a national tour and productions on ABC radio and television. At the same time a revival of *The Slaughter of St Teresa's Day* at the Community Theatre, Sydney, led to a new national interest in the play. *Mates* was first performed in Sydney in 1975 and *Trespassers Will Be Prosecuted* in 1976.

A Hard God became the first part of a trilogy entitled *The Cassidy Album*, of which *Furtive Love* is the second play and *An Eager Hope* the third. The trilogy was performed in its entirety in Adelaide and Sydney in 1978.

In 1973 Peter Kenna received a three-year fellowship from the Literature Board of the Australia Council. He died in 1987.

For Michael Frost.

Mates was first performed at the Nimrod Theatre, Sydney on 1 August 1975 with the following cast:

PERCE	Don Crosby
SYLVIA	Jon Ewing
MABEL	Maggie Blinco
GARY	Peter Fisher

Director, John Bell
Designer, Larry Eastwood

CHARACTERS

PERCE
SYLVIA
MABEL
GARY

SETTING

A cabaret at night. Tables and chairs are loosely arranged, quite close together and littered with the remains of drinks and full ashtrays. The back wall is draped in a heavy dark red fabric which is meant to create an impression of discreet luxury, but it has been polluted by the atmosphere and looks merely sad. A section of a bar is visible downstage right. There is a telephone on the end of it.

The cabaret is in near darkness. PERCE, *hardly visible, stands beside the telephone. He is a man of 65, dressed in out-of-style sportswear which hangs loosely on his spare frame. A shaft of light from a quickly opened doorway stabs across the area and* SYLVIA *appears from left, carrying a balloon of brandy. He is a man in his middle 30s dressed in a loose robe and high-heeled shoes. He moves dejectedly across the stage and exits right.* PERCE *watches him. In a moment, a coin is heard dropping into a juke box slot and a softly orchestrated samba begins.* SYLVIA *re-enters, swaying to the music.* PERCE *moves forward.*

PERCE: Excuse me, love.
SYLVIA: Oh my God!
PERCE: I'm sorry if—
SYLVIA: Oh Jesus, you gave me a fright.
PERCE: I came up the stairs and the place was in darkness ...
SYLVIA: We've been closed two hours.
PERCE: [*looking about*] Yeah, but what is it up here now?
SYLVIA: [*sharply*] What do you mean, what is it?
PERCE: Well, I used to come here before and it was different.
SYLVIA: I wouldn't know about that. Now it's a club and we're closed.
PERCE: [*turning away*] Ah, well. I'm sorry if I gave you a fright. [*Turning back again*] Eh, you're not a real girl, are you?
SYLVIA: [*defiantly*] No.
PERCE: What sort of a club is it, then?
SYLVIA: We do a drag show here.
PERCE: [*grimly*] Oh. [*Nicely*] I didn't mean no offence.

SYLVIA: The management takes none. Now if you wouldn't mind slamming the door as you go out.
PERCE: [*gazing about with renewed interest*] Imagine that. I've never been in one of these places before.
SYLVIA: [*in mock wonder*] Really?
PERCE: What's keeping you here so late?
SYLVIA: I'm waiting for a friend, if you must know. [*Half to himself*] He was supposed to pick me up after the show and he hasn't turned up.
PERCE: [*sympathetically*] Oh.
SYLVIA: [*defiantly*] As a matter of fact he's my lover.
PERCE: [*impressed*] Oh.

> SYLVIA *sighs, irritated by his own performance.*

SYLVIA: I'm sorry, I didn't mean to shock you.
PERCE: [*nicely, turning to go again*] I shouldn't have intruded.
SYLVIA: [*moving after him a little*] Look. It's just that I'm disappointed and a bit miserable. I'm going to wait here a while longer if you'd like to stay and have a look around.
PERCE: Thanks. But I can see now it isn't what I was after. Everything changes, I don't know why I took it for granted this place would be the same. Funny, you watch yourself getting older, your eyes sinking back into your head and your ribs poking out through your skin—but the things in your imagination, you don't expect them to alter, do you?
SYLVIA: I've never thought about it. You're from the bush, aren't you?
PERCE: [*wryly*] How'd you guess? I come down for a couple of weeks every second year. Used to come down regular once a year when I was younger and had a big shearing cheque in

my pocket. But, I don't know, there doesn't seem to be the same interest here now. Oh, I expect that's me. Anyhow, now I just come down for the change.

SYLVIA [*gesturing with his drink*] I have some more brandy in my dressing room if you'd like a drink.

PERCE: [*backing away*] Oh ... no. No.

SYLVIA: You'll be quite safe here, really you will.

PERCE: No, it's not that. It's just—[*Reconsidering*] Well, yeah. I would like a drink.

SYLVIA: Okay, I'll get it. [*Moving away and then turning back*] You will still be here when I get back, won't you?

PERCE: [*puzzled*] Sure.

SYLVIA: All of a sudden this seemed so improbable. Like a scene out of a movie. [*Dramatising wryly*] You know: there's this beautiful girl alone in a nightclub early in the morning, her lover hasn't arrived to pick her up and she realises it's all over between them. Several times she's had the razor blade at her wrist but something, just something, holds her back. Then she decides she simply must hear their favourite song once more. She goes to the juke box and, as she's slipping the ten cents into the slot, this voice speaks to her out of the darkness. It's an old man. A homespun philosopher. The sort of role they used to offer to Frank Craven. Well, she gets talking to him and he's so wise and so ... so spiritual she somehow gains the strength to go on. The near fatal moment has passed. He offers to escort her home and she slips away to fix her make-up. But, when she returns, he's vanished. Now who was he really? Or was he there at all? Was he perhaps her Guardian Angel? She'll never know. And it's going to worry the hell out of her for years.

PERCE: [*scratching his head*] I don't know any Frank Craven.
SYLVIA: It doesn't matter. Just stay where you are until I get back.

> SYLVIA *moves off left.* PERCE *takes a pouch of tobacco from his pocket and rolls a cigarette, considering what has just occurred, nodding to himself and chuckling.* MABEL *enters from right, moving slowly as if climbing the stairs has been difficult. She is not much younger than* PERCE *and takes a great deal of trouble over her appearance in a not-very-well-thought-out campaign to hold off the ravages of time. She is most respectably dressed in rather expensive clothing. She sees* PERCE *and stands regarding him suspiciously. Eventually he feels her presence and turns around.*

PERCE: Oh. Good morning.
MABEL: [*curtly*] Morning.
PERCE: [*after a moment*] Er, the place is closed.
MABEL: I know. I work here.
PERCE: Oh. Are you another one of the—
MABEL: [*thundering*] I am not!
PERCE: Sorry. There isn't much light in here.
MABEL: Would you mind if I inquired what you're doing here?
PERCE: [*confused now*] Well, I used to often come in in the old days when it was—well, I came in a while ago and there was this … chap. And he was waiting for another … chap. Who hadn't arrived. So he asked me to stay and have a drink with him.
MABEL: [*accusingly*] Oh. A tate-a-tate, eh?
PERCE: Look, I've never been in here before. Not since it's changed. Like I said, I used to come here when—

MABEL: You don't have to explain yourself to me, mate. It's none of my business. I just sweep the floor and keep the place clean. It's not up to me to make moral judgements.
PERCE: But I wouldn't want you to think—
MABEL: I told you I don't think anything. They don't pay me to think. [*Removing her coat and turning to go off right again*] Though you don't look the type to me.
PERCE: Oh dear. Oh dear. [*Moving after her*] Look, Mrs—
MABEL: [*turning to him again*] Miss!
PERCE: Yes, well, I just want to say, if you want to tidy up in here let us know and we'll move somewhere else.
MABEL: I see nothing, hear nothing. But the foyer is as far away as I can get.

She moves off right.

PERCE: [*desperately*] Oh dear. Oh dear.

He fidgets in indecision for a moment, then takes up his tobacco pouch and moves to go. SYLVIA *returns. He has taken some of his make-up off and changed into casual male attire. His manner is now more masculine. He carries a bottle of brandy and a grip bag containing, among other things, tissues, cold cream and a mirror. He stops short, seeing* PERCE *retreating.*

SYLVIA: Oh, I am disappointed in you.
PERCE: [*turning back*] Yeah, well, look, I would like to stay but—
SYLVIA: I mean, if you're going to disappear you might at least go up through the ceiling.
PERCE: What are you talking about?

SYLVIA: [*unpacking the bag onto a table*] Only nonsense. I'm feeling a lot better, you see. And I've come to a decision.

PERCE: Look, there was a lady in here—

SYLVIA: Not someone else?

PERCE: She said she works here.

SYLVIA: Oh, that'd be Mabel. You don't have to worry about her.

PERCE: But I think she thought I—

SYLVIA: It doesn't matter what she thinks. She's an old pro.

PERCE: [*slightly reassured*] Oh, is she?

SYLVIA: She'd be still on the game if she could get anybody interested. In fact she might even consider giving it away free. [*Reconsidering*] But, no. Not Mabel. She's too mean for that.

PERCE: It was all right when I thought there was just the two of us—

SYLVIA: You don't mind if I take the rest of my make-up off in here, do you? [*Sipping his drink and nodding towards the bottle*] Oh. Pour yours as you like it.

PERCE: Thanks.

> *He takes a glass from the bar and pours a decent nip of brandy. He throws it down in a gulp and pours another.*

Just make sure we stay in the light where she can see us.

SYLVIA: [*moving to the telephone with his drink*] She'll make sure she sees us.

> *He dials a number. After a long moment he is answered and speaks.*

Listen, you bastard, I'm still at the club waiting for you. Now listen, I don't want any interruptions until I've had my say. I am standing here with a razor blade in my hand and in exactly ten minutes I'm going to cut my wrists with it. While I am waiting for the time to pass I intend to sit down and write a letter to the coach of your football team telling him everything. So much for your precious bloody reputation. When the letter is finished I shall take it downstairs and post it, take a last look around at the world outside, and then come back here and finish the whole thing off. Ten minutes! You might spare me a thought if you haven't gone back to sleep by then. Cheerio. It's been a fucking pleasure knowing you.

He hangs up and breathes out in relief.

I think he'll arrive in about seven minutes, don't you?

PERCE: [*his mouth agape*] But you're not going to—you didn't mean—

SYLVIA: Actually, I was considering it just before you arrived but now I'm too wild. I've never heard of anybody committing suicide when they're furious.

PERCE: Well, he's going to be pretty bloody cranky when he gets here, isn't he? I mean if you haven't—

SYLVIA: I'm certainly not going to go through with it just to make his trip over here worthwhile. Anyhow, whatever happens it's got to be settled tonight once and for all. I can't go on like this any longer.

He sits at the table and finishes removing his make-up. PERCE stares at him in amazement.

PERCE: Can I take it from what you said on the telephone that this friend of yours is a footballer?

SYLVIA: [*proudly*] Oh yes. One of the big professionals.
PERCE: And how long have you been … ? If it's not a rude question.
SYLVIA: Let's see. He came in to see the show about eight weeks ago. We do two a night. One at eleven and another at one o'clock. They were at the first. A whole team of them. Apparently they'd won that day and came in for a dare. They were a rowdy lot, stamping around sending everybody up; we were relieved when they left. But, guess what? He was back again for the second show. By himself. And he waited around afterwards. And we got into conversation. And then I went back to his place with him.
PERCE: I suppose that dressed up like a girl and all—
SYLVIA: I wasn't dressed up like a girl after the show. And he certainly didn't expect me to behave like one. Exactly the opposite. Well, after that we just went on seeing each other and the first month was terrific. Sometimes he'd come back to my place and we'd laugh and eat and muck about. We never made arrangements to keep it going. Oh no. That way it was like every time was going to be the last and so we made the most of it. But then, about two weeks ago, something happened. He was driving me home and we stopped for a traffic light and someone waved to him from another car. Apparently that was all it needed. He blushed to the roots of his hair and the light changed to green again without him even noticing. He'd been caught with me, you see, and he's never been the same since. He gets later and later picking me up and some nights he'll ring and leave a message for me to take a taxi over there. Now, I'm not a fool. Usually when that sort of thing starts to happen you can see the writing on the

wall. They might as well pick up a violin and start playing 'God Save the Queen'. But this time it's not as simple as that. I know he isn't getting tired of me. It's just who he is and what people would say if they found out about us. And maybe ... maybe he can't bear needing me as much as he does.

PERCE: Well. A footballer. You'd never credit it.

SYLVIA: Like I say, it isn't all physical. We're friends too.

PERCE: Like mates.

SYLVIA: That's right.

PERCE: Oh well, I ought to know a bit about that. I've had dozens of mates myself. Been pretty close to some of them too. A couple I'd have cut my arm off for. But, going beyond that—well—it's unthinkable.

SYLVIA: It's a question of what you need, I suppose.

PERCE: I know that when you're out on the road walking from one job to the next, a good mate can mean the difference between a dog's life and a king's. He's company for you and you can split the work so you're bedded down earlier and off on the track again before the sun gets too high. A good mate can become like another part of yourself really. There was one particular bloke I travelled with for, oh, quite a few seasons. Parkhill. Now, this sort of thing used to happen all the time: we'd be sitting by the fire where we'd camped for the night and we'd have had our tucker and we'd be drawing on our cigarettes. You know, nice and still and the bush quiet all around you. Just the sound of the fire crackling and your lips sucking the tobacco. And this tune might come into my head. And I'd draw in my breath to start humming it and bugger me dead if at exactly the same moment he wouldn't blow out his breath and start whistling it. That's how close you can get to another man.

SYLVIA: And never any closer?

PERCE: Not a chance in the world. Though, naturally, you discuss sex quite a lot. Men always will when they're alone together to, sort of, compare performances. There was another mate I had. Chapman. One night we clicked with these two girls in a pub at Forbes. Well, we didn't have anywhere to go and they was sharing a room together so that's where we all ended up. A pair of us in each bed. We were young fellas and hot-blooded and, God knows, they was eager enough. Before long we were banging away at it with the lights on and all. After a bit I looked around to see how old Chapman was going and there he was just lying beside his girl stroking her and watching me doing it. And there was this wistful look on his face. I've never forgotten it. [*Confidentially*] Of course I know what it was. He was a big fella you see but [*crooking his little finger*] that was about all he had. [*Proudly*] And I certainly wasn't behind the door when they was passing them out. It was envy, that's all. And later on when I thought about it I felt quite sorry for him. But it would have been insulting to say anything of course.

SYLVIA: I've been with girls too, you know. I was even engaged once.

PERCE: Never!

SYLVIA: I was a lot younger and she was more keen on me than I was on her. But we used to have sex and all. Though it was more like gymnastics. There was no love to it.

PERCE: Well, frankly, I've never had any particularly strong feelings for women myself. I must have had hundreds of them in my time. And I've been damn fond of some of them. And good to all of them, I hope. But I've never really known what they was talking about when they talked about love. I've just enjoyed myself going through them one after the other. [*Chuckling*] Gawd, I was a randy young bugger. [*Wistfully*] I'd be at it still if I could manage it.

SYLVIA: Oh, you're not that old.

PERCE: I suppose the blood gets thinner in some than in others. And I've lived a hard life. It takes its toll. The excitement isn't there any more.

SYLVIA: Do you miss it?

PERCE: Well, let's put it this way, I'd miss it a lot more if I felt like it and couldn't get it. That's why I came round here tonight, because all of a sudden I did want it.

SYLVIA: But ... why here?

PERCE: Well, that's what this place used to be. It used to be a brothel.

SYLVIA: Oh! Now I remember. Somebody did say something once.

PERCE: [*fondly*] Oh, it was a lovely place. I don't want to run down what it is now but honest, it couldn't be a patch on what it used to be like. There was a small parlour out in the front with a couple of sofas and some soft lights. That's where Madam greeted you to make the arrangements. [*Reverently*] She was a most dignified woman. Some of them will hop in themselves and cope with the customers if there's a bit of a rush but not this madam. She was above it all, serene and ladylike. And there was generally a good class of girl here. They made you welcome. I don't suppose that any of them feel like doing it all the time but they encouraged you to think they did. It was very satisfactory. Oh, this was a long time ago. A whole bunch of us used to roll in here when we came down to the city. Thommo and Carter and Carmichael. Funny buggers. Though, mind you, it wasn't all jokes. Blokes can get pretty touchy when they're out on a rooting binge. Oftentimes a blue'd be in the air when two or more of them wanted the same girl and it was obvious she preferred just one. Then it became a matter of pride and, if a fight did break out, it was a bloody violent one. Like they was battling to protect their virility. Funny buggers! I'm talking too much, aren't I?

SYLVIA: You go it while you can. I don't think you'll get much of a chance once Gary gets here.

PERCE: It's the grog. Always makes me talk.

SYLVIA: Is that why you felt so lively tonight? Were you drinking before you came here?

PERCE: No. These days I can't come at that too much either. These days I'm generally stone cold sober and in bed by ten thirty. I certainly was tonight. What worked me up so much was that I had this dream. Not that it was about sex exactly. I mean there was no women in it. It was just myself. And I was young again, you see, and had all my strength back. By God it was vivid. I was in a shearing shed and I was the ringer just like I used to be before. They'd keep pushing the ewes at me and I'd grip them between my knees and run the clippers through their lovely soft fleeces. Then away with that one and take hold of another. It was as easy as dancing. The other poor bastards were turning themselves inside out and not even approaching my tally. Now, although I wasn't tired I was running with sweat and I called for some water and they brought it to me, a great pitcher of it. And I poured it over my head and watched it run down my body—over my arms with the veins pulsing just under the skin, down my chest and stomach and into my trousers. But it didn't cool me. Not on your life. My body warmed it. And I got hotter and hotter until I started to glow. God it was good. And then I woke up.

SYLVIA: Oh, so this place didn't come into your dream at all?

PERCE: No. But I was thinking of it as I came to. It was in my mind then. And I was so excited I got up and turned on the light. And what do you think?

SYLVIA: What?

PERCE slaps his hand against the inside of his elbow and thrusts his clenched fist upwards.

PERCE: It was like that.

SYLVIA: [*gently mocking*] Good God!

PERCE: In fact all of me was full of that sort of energy. My wrinkles seemed to have vanished and the little aches and pains I'd felt creeping on me for years were gone too. I wasn't a new man. I was the old one, fully restored. And I was so bloody delighted I got dressed as quick as I could and raced around here. You'd have thought that once I'd hit the fresh air I'd have woken up properly, but I didn't. Only when I reached the top of those stairs, only when I saw how this place was all changed, that's when I woke up. And I went as limp as a used French letter.

SYLVIA: Look, there must be other places around here you could go.

PERCE: No. It's too late now. This place was part of it, you see. The feeling depended on it.

SYLVIA: Oh, what a pity.
PERCE: Never mind. I should have known. You can't turn back the clock.

> MABEL *comes in again, sweeping the floor She is now wearing a smart nylon dustcoat and has her elaborately coiffed hair wrapped in a transparent chiffon scarf.*

MABEL: Oh hello, Sylvia love. It's you still here.
SYLVIA: Hello, Mabel. That bloody Gary's stood me up.
MABEL: No! He ought to be knackered. Not that it's any of my business, I suppose.
SYLVIA: You've met— [*To* PERCE] What is your name, by the way?
PERCE: Perce.
MABEL: [*stonily*] Oh yes.
SYLVIA: Mabel's been around here a long time, she might know when that place you was talking about closed down. Mabel, do you remember when this place used to be a house?
MABEL: Indeed I do, dear. As a matter of fact I often worked here myself.
PERCE: You don't say!
SYLVIA: Isn't that incredible? That's why Perce came round here tonight. He thought it might still be here.
MABEL: [*relieved and delighted*] Oh, really?

> *She drops her broom and moves to* PERCE, *all charm.*

Oh, yes. Unfortunately it closed down years ago. [*Reverently*] Madam developed a growth in her breast, you know, and it killed her.
PERCE: [*reverently back to her*] No, I didn't know.

MABEL: Such a fine woman.
PERCE: [*excitedly*] That's what I was telling … Sylvia here. Didn't I say that?
SYLVIA: You did indeed, Perce. Just think, you two might have been off together half a dozen times and you didn't even recognise each other.
PERCE: Well, it was a long time ago, wasn't it, Mabel?
MABEL: It was. And the best of times as far as I'm concerned. I really used to like being here. It was different from some of the other places you was forced into. It was somehow … cosier.
PERCE: [*to* SYLVIA] And I said that too, didn't I? [*To* MABEL] Look, there was generally five of us used to come in here together. Carter and Thommo and Carmichael … and … and White. And myself. Of course, I looked a bit different then to how I look now but Carter was a tall, fair-headed fella with freckles. And Thommo, he was red-haired and … pudgy. And White was blond too but smaller than Carter with a cast in one eye.
MABEL: [*thoughtfully*] Oh yes. I think … I think they do ring a bell.
SYLVIA: [*laughing*] Oh, Mabel, stop it. You don't remember one of them.
MABEL: [*firmly*] Well, I wish I did.
PERCE: Oh, aren't I a silly old bugger! All the hundreds of people you had coming through here, why should you remember just five of us? Pretty ordinary looking blokes at that.
MABEL: [*touching him gently and lying*] Never mind, love, I liked you all. Particularly the bushies.
PERCE: [*eager again*] Honest?

MABEL: Honest and true. You needed it so bad, you see. It was like handing a thirsty man a drink.

PERCE: [*formally*] Thank you, Mabel. It's very kind of you to express it in that manner. And, you know, we only remembered you for about six months. We'd ask all the girls their names, you see, and when we got back to the sheds we'd compare notes.

MABEL: Cheeky things!

PERCE: But after the first couple of weeks, it got right out of hand. One or another of us would start inventing things to keep up with the others and then we'd get all the names confused, so that even if we met you again the year after, it might as well have been a different Shirley or Gladys or Mabel.

MABEL: Oh well, I don't know whether I like that very much. Mind you, we didn't suppose you'd remember us forever, but I don't know whether I like the idea of you confusing us with one another. There was a couple of girls here I wouldn't have wanted to be confused with.

PERCE: Oh yes. I remember one in particular. A big, fat, dark looking girl we used to avoid.

MABEL: Oh, that'd be big, black Myra.

PERCE: That's it. That was her name. Myra. Thommo took her on one night. I think he'd lost a bet or something. Well, did he have a time! She got him into the room and tried to talk him out of it. She said how would he feel if it was his own sister in the position she was in. God, it cut him up. She had a point, I suppose, but she made him feel bloody dreadful. He never came down here with us again for the rest of his stay.

MABEL: Oh yes, she could be disgraceful to the customers.

[*Reverently*] Madam had to speak to her severely on several occasions. But I'll say this for her: she had a good heart and what they call nowadays a social conscience.
PERCE: Well, that's all right. But a social conscience wasn't what poor bloody Thommo was paying for.

They laugh. GARY *hurtles headlong into the room. He is in a state of desperation and stops dead at seeing the little party in progress. They turn to him and stop laughing,* SYLVIA *with his brandy balloon poised in the air.* GARY's *desperation turns to wrath.* SYLVIA *lowers his head and places the balloon on the table, ashamed of being caught out so badly.*

GARY: [*through clenched teeth*] You bloody lying queen!

He rushes to SYLVIA *and shakes him, grunting savagely.* SYLVIA *closes his eyes and surrenders to the chastisement.* PERCE *and* MABEL *attempt to drag* GARY *away, both speaking at once.*

PERCE: Oh come on now, this is no way to behave. Calm down.
MABEL: I'm not going to have any violence in here. If you're going to fight I'm going to call the police.

GARY *releases* SYLVIA *and breaks away from* PERCE *and* MABEL. *He flops down at another table and buries his head in his arms, weeping hysterically.* GARY *is a strongly built, good-looking man in his early 20s. The others stare at him,* SYLVIA *in sorrow,* PERCE *in embarrassment and* MABEL *in puzzlement.*

PERCE: [*quietly*] Oh dear, oh dear.
MABEL: [*to* SYLVIA] I thought it was him stood you up.

> SYLVIA *moves to* GARY *and tentatively places his hand on his arm.*

SYLVIA: Gary, don't cry like that.

> GARY *springs to life again and slaps* SYLVIA *across the face with his open hand.*

GARY: Fucking lying queen!

> *Again* SYLVIA *accepts the blow.* PERCE *and* MABEL *step forward to assist him, but he stays them with a gesture.* GARY *is now standing with his hands on the table, breathing heavily. The act of slapping* SYLVIA *has begun to relieve his tension.*

I nearly had a crash getting over here. I came into the main road and sideswiped a Ford. I put my foot down and got out of it as quick as I could but, if they took my number, I'm a goner. [*To* PERCE *and* MABEL] Well? What are you two staring at?

> PERCE *lowers his eyes.* MABEL *bustles about the room removing ashtrays from the tables and placing them on the bar.* SYLVIA *sits at a table close to* GARY *and watches him.* PERCE *now decides on a direct approach to defuse the situation. He moves to* GARY *with his hand extended.*

PERCE: My name's Perce Whitticker. I was out at the footie on Saturday as a matter of fact, and I recognised you the minute you walked in. [*Taking* GARY*'s hand and placing it in his own*] Put it there, boy. You're the best bloody winger I've ever seen. The blokes in the shed will be tickled pink when I tell them I met up with you down here.

> GARY *gazes at him in horror for a moment, then turns*

away with his hand over his face in a belated gesture of concealment.

GARY: Oh Jesus! [*Hissing at* SYLVIA] What are you trying to do to me?

SYLVIA: I can't help it if you're well-known.

PERCE: Oh, I wouldn't let on I'd met up with you here. No, honest. I know how to keep my mouth shut.

GARY: I'm sure you do … until you get a few drinks under your belt. Then it'll make the best bloody story in the world.

PERCE returns to his table, hurt and angry.

SYLVIA: He's a very nice fella. He was only trying to help.

GARY: [*hissing*] Get him out of here, will you? Get them both out.

PERCE: [*rising again, to* SYLVIA] Err, where's the … ?

SYLVIA: Through that door over there, Perce.

PERCE exits left with a show of dignity. MABEL *remains resolutely where she is.* SYLVIA *and* GARY *turn and stare at her but this only has the effect of making her movements more elaborate, as if she is playing to a large audience.*

Mabel, do you think you could find something else to do for a moment, love?

MABEL: [*as though surprised*] Umm? Well, I've finished in the foyer. I mean, I am the only one supposed to be here, you know.

SYLVIA: What about the dressing rooms? You haven't done those yet.

MABEL: [*taking up her broom peevishly*] Well, they won't take me long. I don't want to poke my nose in where I'm not wanted, of course. I don't enjoy the spectacle of grown men behaving like hysterical housewives.

She exits left.

GARY: Oh Jesus! Why didn't you stand in the street and sell tickets before I arrived?

SYLVIA: [*beginning to fight back*] Look, you were supposed to pick me up after the last show. I waited for you and waited for you and, okay, I got a bit hysterical myself. Why didn't you pick me up, by the way?

GARY: I just … decided I wouldn't.

SYLVIA: You could have rung and left a message.

GARY: And my name.

SYLVIA: You've done it before. You think they don't know who you are by now?

GARY: Yes, I'll bet you've seen to that. God! What have I been thinking of?

SYLVIA: Me, I'd hoped.

GARY: That's right. You've kept me moving so fast I haven't had time to see where I was.

SYLVIA: [*hurt*] Thank you.

GARY: Look, Neil, I just can't go on with it. It's too risky. If anybody on the team found out I was coming down here … What about those two? You think they're going to keep their mouths shut about what they've seen here tonight?

SYLVIA: They wouldn't be here to see anything if you had picked me up as we'd—

GARY: Will you stop going on and bloody on about me not picking you up? Why didn't you go home when I didn't arrive? That's what I would have done.

SYLVIA: [*lost for a reasonable answer*] I—I couldn't believe you'd let me down. I trusted you.
GARY: Oh yes! Ringing me up at four o'clock in the morning with bloody suicide threats.
SYLVIA: Had you decided you weren't going to see me again … ever?
GARY: I don't know. I just wanted to forget about everything. I didn't want to have to worry any more.
SYLVIA: Well, if you'd made that clear to me I wouldn't have bothered you. If that is what you want—
GARY: It is. It has to be.
SYLVIA: Okay. Let's forget it then.

> GARY *sits down heavily.* SYLVIA *assumes a nonchalant air and fiddles with the tissues and cold cream on the table. After a moment* GARY *looks at him in anguish.*

GARY: Oh sure! But what am I going to do about what's happened already? How can I keep that quiet?
SYLVIA: Well, don't ask me. Get married quickly. People'll think twice before they say anything then.
GARY: Yes, I suppose that'd be one way out of it.
SYLVIA: Have you anybody in mind?
GARY: Oh, there's a couple of girls I'm interested in.
SYLVIA: Good luck to you then. Send me a piece of the wedding cake.

> GARY *glances at him.* SYLVIA *sees the lie in his eyes, moves across the room and stands boldly in front of him.* GARY *lowers his head. There is a long pause as they remain rigidly as they are. Then* GARY *reaches out and takes* SYLVIA's *hand in both his own. He presses the palm*

of it to his lips and begins weeping again, this time softly.
SYLVIA caresses his head.

There are no girls, are there?

GARY: None that I want. I stay out of their way as much as I can, but that doesn't stop them following me up. And then I have to think of all these ridiculous excuses to piss them off. Other women waiting at home, religious convictions. I told a couple of them I had gonorrhoea. How can I just say I'm not interested? They'd start working it out for themselves if I did.

SYLVIA: Oh Gary, you can't go on like that.

GARY: It's you I want. And there's no way in the world I can have you.

SYLVIA: If you wanted me enough you'd find a way.

GARY: [*angrily, rising and moving away*] What way? Don't be bloody stupid. Have you any idea of what's expected of me? I can't go anywhere without being recognised. Little kids shake my hand proudly. I get letters from their mothers saying they hope they'll grow up to be just like me. People ask my opinion about this or that and I'm expected to come up with the answer they want to hear every time. I'm good at playing football, that's all. I didn't ask for the rest of it. It's been forced on me and there's no way I can walk away from it.

SYLVIA: But it isn't going to go on forever, is it? Eventually you won't have to worry about walking away, they'll lose interest in you. Is that when you plan to start being yourself? When nobody gives a damn who you are? Well, I'm not hanging around till then.

GARY: If it was possible to keep it quiet. If you worked any place but here.
SYLVIA: No. You'd find it easier to deceive people, that's all. You wouldn't be any more content with what you are yourself.
GARY: [*threateningly*] What am I? What do you think I am?
SYLVIA: [*evasively*] I think you're a fool for not taking what you want when it's offered to you.
GARY: Don't give me any of that shit. How would you be affected if people did find out about us? You'd get a bit more publicity for your act, that's all. And, talking about deceiving people, what do you think you're doing mincing around that stage every night dressed as a woman?
SYLVIA: [*suddenly furious*] They know I'm not a woman and, by Christ, so do you. You've got to deceive even yourself by making me dress up as a girl to fuck you.

> GARY *glances desperately at the dressing rooms and then back to* SYLVIA. *He gathers himself into a ball of rage to attack him.* SYLVIA *sees the danger and moves quickly behind a table.*

Gary, don't!

> GARY *brings himself under control once more.*

GARY: [*quietly and desperately*] You merciless little bastard! I'd cut my tongue out before I'd whisper that to anyone and you ... you shout it out for the cleaning lady and some barfly to hear.
SYLVIA: I'm sorry. It was what you said about me dressing up. I'm a man too, you know, and it's as important to me as it is to

you. When you're embarrassed at being seen with me, when you're terrified that someone is going to find out that we even know each other, then you take that away from me. And it hurts. But I'm sorry for what I said. Forgive me. Please.
GARY: No.
SYLVIA: You're looking for an excuse to walk out on me, aren't you?
GARY: If I was you've certainly given it to me.
SYLVIA: And what am I expected to do after you're gone? Come on, you're generous enough with everybody else, give me the answer I want to hear.
GARY: I figure you'll get over it.
SYLVIA: Oh yes, of course I will. I always do. And I'm always just that little bit less human afterwards. Well, do you know something? I've had getting over it. This time I want someone to stay. I want you to stay.

> PERCE *re-enters from left and pauses, realising he has intruded again.*

PERCE: [*to make the best of it*] You know, that Mabel's a cheeky old piece but she's got a better memory than I gave her credit for. She just pinched me on the bum as I passed her.
SYLVIA: [*bitterly*] Congratulations, Perce. That's a better offer than I've had all evening.

> *He exits quickly left.* GARY *is lost for a moment, then turns to* PERCE.

GARY: [*courteously*] Look, I'm sorry about when I came in. I was upset but I shouldn't have taken it out on you.
PERCE: Don't worry about it. I said to Sylvia when he made that phone call, I said you'd be cranky when you got here.

GARY: Yeah, well, I was.

PERCE: And you know, you don't have to worry about me gossiping. I do know how to keep a secret. As a matter of fact, I'm carrying confidences [*touching his heart*] in here that were put there by people when I was a kid. A lot of them are dead and buried now and it wouldn't matter who I told. But I never will. Because a secret is a secret.

GARY: Well, thanks.

PERCE: And would you mind if I gave you a bit of advice? I was thinking it out while I was sitting on the lav back there waiting for the time to pass. You don't want to feel badly about what's happened between you and [*nodding off*] him. Even out of girl's clothes I can imagine he might be attractive to a lot of fairly fair dinkum blokes. And you never ought to feel ashamed of what you really want. It's no use. You want it and that's all there is about it. I went for a sheila covered in tattoos once. Saw her in a sideshow and simply had to have her. You'd never believe it, she had the wreck of the Hesperus on one tit and Grace Darling rowing out to save the crew on the other. And, when I got her bloomers off her, there was Nelson saying, 'Kiss me, Hardy' all over her twat. She was mad about the Navy. Now most people would have found that repulsive, but I didn't. And that's what I want to tell you. Providing you don't hurt other people, take what you want out of life. In the long run it's the only thing that'll make you happy.

MABEL: [*urgently, off*] Perce! Could you give us a bit of a hand here?

    PERCE *and* GARY *rise, alarmed by the sound of her voice.*

She appears, supporting SYLVIA, *who looks pale and is faint. He presses a blood-stained handkerchief to his wrist.* GARY *freezes.* PERCE *bustles over to help* MABEL *support* SYLVIA.

PERCE: What's happened?

MABEL: Oh, the silly little bugger scratched at his wrist with a razor blade.

SYLVIA: I'm all right.

MABEL: Of course you are, dear. [*To* PERCE] He hasn't done much damage.

They sit SYLVIA *in a chair and* MABEL *lifts and replaces the handkerchief quickly.*

MABEL: I think the bleeding's just about stopped.

GARY *has seen the cut. His stomach heaves. He slaps his hand over his mouth and runs off left.*

MABEL: Well, you can forget about that one in a crisis.

SYLVIA: [*rising*] Is he all right? Go and see if he's all right, Perce.

MABEL: Never you mind about him. You think about yourself, because the next time you try that you might succeed.

SYLVIA: No, I don't want to try it again. I didn't realise it would hurt so much.

PERCE: It's the coward's way out, Sylvia.

SYLVIA: Yes, Perce.

MABEL: Now, you take notice of what he's saying because he's right. My God, if I'd done myself in the number of times I've felt like it I'd have had to have been a cat with nine lives. And six months afterwards do you think I had any idea of what made me want to do it? Oh, sometimes it might have been a broken love affair and sometimes it was simply a hard trot. Who knows? And, from where I'm standing I certainly don't care. So, you take my advice, Sylvia. You plan to die in bed. With someone beside you if possible.

SYLVIA: Even as I was doing it I was thinking I didn't want to die. And the answer to everything seemed so simple. All I have to do is change myself so that Gary won't be ashamed of me. And I will. I'll get out of this place for a start. I'll find a job somewhere else. Something steady. And I'll go to those bloody awful football games too. I'll sit in the stands and cheer my head off even though I won't have the slightest idea what I'm cheering about. All that matters is how I feel about him. [*Rising again*] Where is he?

As SYLVIA *moves left,* GARY *enters, wiping his mouth with a handkerchief and carrying a band-aid. They pause and gaze at each other in relief.*

GARY: [*fondly*] You bloody stupid fool.

SYLVIA: I know. I know I am. Are you all right?

GARY: Get rid of that handkerchief. [*Giving the band-aid to* MABEL] Here. Put this on the cut for him, will you?

MABEL *applies the band-aid to* SYLVIA'*s wrist, cleaning the traces of blood away with spittle and a finger. She tucks the offending handkerchief in her dust-coat pocket.*

MABEL: There.

GARY: Right. Now come on, I'll take you round to the hospital.

SYLVIA: Oh, I don't want to go to the hospital, Gary. It's only a scratch.

GARY: [*peeved*] You're going to need an anti-tetanus injection, aren't you? Where did you get the razor blade from? I suppose one of those other queens had been using it to shave her crutch with.

SYLVIA: No. It was new. I took it out of the antiseptic wrapper not a second before I used it.

GARY: Don't argue with me, just come on.

SYLVIA: Oh, all right. Mabel, love, would you put that cold cream and stuff back in the dressing room for me?

MABEL: I'll fix it.

GARY: [*suddenly*] Oh Jesus! How can I take you into a hospital to get treatment for a suicide attempt? They'll recognise me straight away.

SYLVIA: [*wearily*] Oh, very well then, don't take me. I think I'd rather have the tetanus anyway.

GARY: Listen, all I'm asking you to do is walk into the casualty by yourself. I'll wait around the corner in the car.

SYLVIA: Fine. I'll go into the wardrobe and get you a big black hat with a veil.

GARY: Don't you start again. By Christ, don't you start again.

SYLVIA: [*immediately penitent*] Oh no. I'm sorry. Yes. Yes. You wait around the corner in the car.

GARY: [*reasonably*] Of course if you don't feel well enough to walk in—

SYLVIA: I do. I do. And listen, I'll tell them a broken glass did it. I mean it doesn't look like a suicide attempt. Why don't you just drop me there and I'll get a cab back to your place afterwards.

GARY: No, no. I'll wait around the corner.

SYLVIA: All right. Whatever you say. I mean it. Whatever you say. [*Extending his hand to* PERCE] Goodbye, Perce. It's been a real pleasure meeting you. Why don't you come and see the show before you go back?

PERCE: [*nothing would induce him*] I might ... yes ... I might.

MABEL: [*sagely*] Now, you be careful, Sylvia. I don't want to intrude, but ... you be careful.

> SYLVIA *smiles to her reassuringly.* GARY *nods and they begin to move off right. At the door,* SYLVIA *pauses and looks back, having forgotten his grip bag.* GARY *courteously returns for it and, placing his arm about* SYLVIA's *shoulders, escorts him from the room.*

Of course it's not for me to comment, but I'll be surprised if they make the car without him trying to strangle her again.

PERCE: Well, now that they're gone, I suppose I'd better be thinking of getting along myself.

MABEL: Oh, you don't have to run off yet, do you, Perce?

PERCE: I suppose I could stay and finish the bottle. Will you have one with me, Mabel?

MABEL: No. I don't drink. I never have. But I've lost so much time already I may as well sit with you for a while. [*As she sits*] I'll call it a tea break.

> *She gazes at* PERCE *winningly and then presents to him a series of mildly seductive poses which clearly worked wonders in the old days. He acknowledges he is impressed by smiling back and nodding appreciatively.*

Listen, I've got a really good idea. Why don't you stay here until I've finished cleaning up. I can whiz through here in a jiffy if I really try. And then you can come home to my place for breakfast.

PERCE: Yes, that'd really round off the evening, wouldn't it? But … no thanks, Mabel. I'm afraid I'd only disappoint you.

MABEL: Let me be the judge of that. Unless, of course, you don't think I'm pretty enough any more.

PERCE: I think you're a little beauty. It's not that. The sad fact is I can't manage it any more.

MABEL: But I thought Sylvia said you was looking for company when you came around here earlier. What were you looking for?

PERCE: Something I'd left behind me, I suppose. Something I saw again in a dream and thought was here. But it was only a dream.

MABEL: [*after a moment's consideration*] You know what? You're as hard to work out as [*nodding off*] they are. Still, it's never been easy for me to understand men. I've spent the greater part of my life with them in the most intimate of circumstances and yet they're still a mystery to me. However, I don't suppose it's any of my business anyway.

They sit in silence as the lights die about them.

THE END

www.ingramcontent.com/pod-product-compliance
Lightning Source LLC
Chambersburg PA
CBHW050028090426
42734CB00021B/3468